Preserved for a
Purpose:

Surviving the Genocide of
Cambodia
to Thriving in America

Sok-Khieng (So-Can) Lim Hardy

with
Maribeth Slovasky

Author: Sok-Khieng Lim Hardy
Contributor: Maribeth Slovasky
Cover Design: Kelly Cory
Copyright © 2021 by Dockbravlick Distribution
ISBN: 978-0-9996909-3-2

Present for a Purpose

To my kids, Wyatt and Whitney
Don't be perfect as that's boring
and remember to make this world a better place.
Love you!

∞

Present for a Purpose

CONTENTS

Foreword

From the Journal of Davuth Cheng 9.23.2000
Leaving Cambodia Alive

I left our village with my family to attempt to reach Thailand and escape the tyrannical rule of Pol Pot and the Khmer Rouge. I was 13 and my parents and I managed to take what we could from home, walk three days to the Western shore of Cambodia where a boat would take us across the Gulf of Thailand to a Red Cross camp.

My family, like most others in our village, were rice farmers. We heard about the atrocities of Pol Pot's reign and the continued attacks and destruction of our country. Still, with minimal communication we remained free from oppression because of our ignorance. When our village was invaded by Khmer Rouge soldiers, we were forced to give them our rice, abide by their rules and demands, and lose whatever sense of life we once knew. Leaving because my family said to was fine with me.

What I remember about that time still brings nightmares to my sub-conscious mind and continues to remind me that had we not left when we did, there is a good chance I would not be sharing this memory. Did she survive? My mind

ix

believes she did; however, after all these years, I have grown more cynical and uncertain about believing in miracles.

We boarded a wooden fishing boat, found a small corner to sit, and watched as more than 100 others made their way on to the vessel built for 50. I knew that silence and the dark of night were our friends, and I was nervous that there were several young children with us. We left the shore undetected.

The ride in the Gulf of Thailand wasn't long, yet the slow pace the boat had to travel was excruciating. Most of the children onboard were asleep and that kept the noise down. My eyes were closed when I heard the mother of a family near us whisper to her husband that their daughter was no longer in her lap.

សុខនៅឯណា? (Where is Sok?) She sounded frightened.

សុខនៅឯណា? (Where is Sok?) she repeated, this time loud enough to be heard by other passengers.

Several people whispered, ស្ងាត់ (Quiet!) and បញ្ឈប់ (Stop!).

I heard a splash in the water. I thought it was a fish, prayed it was not the enemy, and somehow knew the little girl had fallen in. An audible cry from the mother created a ripple effect, and the boat now was in more danger than I knew.

ទុកឱ្យនាង (Leave her!) expressed several adults in the boat.

They began rowing the boat faster, the silence no longer worth it because we were closer to the shore of Thailand and apparent freedom. The little girl's mother was crying, and her siblings began to wake up and sensed their mother's fear. With all the confusion and dread around, the girl's father went into the water to search for his daughter. I looked over the side and saw a dark shadow near the boat.

នៅទីនោះ! (There!) I said to the man and pointed. He looked my way and began to swim towards where I was pointing. It felt like he was moving in slow motion and when he finally reached the girl, he picked her up, carried her closer to the boat, and I leaned over and took the lifeless body from him.

I handed the toddler to her mother as the other adults around pushed me out of the way. I couldn't see her anymore. The boat was close enough to the shore to hear the call from those waiting to help. My father took my arm and we gathered most of our belongings. Although I didn't understand the significance of the moment as it was happening, freedom felt both exhilarating and comforting.

The confusion that followed kept me focused on staying with my parents. It was the next morning when I realized I had not seen the little girl or her family again. That remains true to this day.

I would like to believe she was taken to a country with her family and grew up to be someone with her own family and a career. We all deserve a chance at life. I hope she got hers.

.

Part One

Refugee Me

Chapter 1
Escaping a Genocide

Running out of ideas will put you in the dark until death. --
Cambodian Proverb

In order to understand why, it's easier to begin with the tangibles. I was barely three years old when my family left our village in Cambodia, and my earliest memories of childhood don't include that time. However fleeing the heinous rule of the Khmer Rouge made it the right decision to leave the only home my family knew.

That boat ride to freedom was preceded by more than one attempt to escape. My mother and her children tried twice before to escape to Thailand and were captured and jailed. I don't remember any of it and often wonder how she was able to endure and how we all lived to reunite with the rest of my family.

It was in 1978 when we boarded an overcrowded wooden boat to travel to nearby Thailand with the hope of being sent to a distant country where we would be "refugees." No one really understood what was happening to us because the war in our country was fought mostly through the stories we heard as people occasionally passed through our village. My father was a fisherman, married a Chinese woman (my mom), and raised his family in the village where he grew up. To pack up and leave was strange and foreboding. Nevertheless, off we went.

When we arrived in Thailand, Red Cross tents were our home for the next few days. My parents, along with the rest of our "family" (their five children and five other members of our village who became "aunts" and "uncles"), were being sent to West Linn, Oregon, USA, to be "adopted" by a church there. Our group was the only one sent to Oregon; the other villagers went to other parts of the U.S., Australia, or France.

 Although we were safe from the horrors of Cambodia, the 12 of us were off to Oregon, the only ones who spoke our language, and what lay ahead seemed as ominous as what we left behind.

∞∞∞∞

Living Your Story

My story begins from someone else's perspective; I was too young for the events to have meaning when they happened. What's your story that gets told from someone else's point of view? Does it bring you happiness? Fear? Joy? Embarrassment? The gift of the stories we all have, no matter what the situation, can bring us a stronger sense of knowing who we are. The lessons we've learned give us the ability to teach others. Regardless of the moment, there are positive lessons to be gained from your past experiences.

Chapter 2
Camping in Thailand (Refugee-style)

We travel not to escape life, but so life doesn't escape us. –
unknown

We were taken from the boat to a Red Cross camp, I think. My family remembers the large, bright red crosses on the top of the tents. We were not the only boat that arrived at camp. Between December 1978 and May 1979, an estimated 30,000 Cambodians had fled to several improvised camps in eastern Thailand.

We were examined by a doctor in preparation for travel and life in a new country. The doctor, who communicated with us through an interpreter, learned that I had fallen in the water and stopped breathing. He explained to my parents that a lack of oxygen to the brain can cause brain damage. He advised my parents to include me on their journey. However, he also said, according to an interpreter, that I "would never function normally." My parents were grateful I was alive.

7

There were three places in the world where we could be relocated: Australia, France, or the United States. Each head of the family chose a ball from a large container that indicated their new home. My family of 12 was the only one sent to the western United States. Mom and Dad were incredibly sad that others from our village would not be joining us; nevertheless, we boarded a plane for the long journey to Portland, Oregon, and our new life as Cambodian refugees.

∞∞∞

Finding Courage

Courage comes to us all. When we know what lies ahead is dangerous or challenging (like walking across a rickety bridge or climbing a rock wall), courage gives us the ability to begin, the adrenaline keeps us going, and the pride we feel at that journey's end makes for a grand adventure!

When we face a task that is unknown, often not a result of our choosing, and includes other people, the experience takes a vastly different tone. If you remember a time in your life that took that kind of courage, I hope you see the growth it brought you. If you are still struggling with a difficult time, remember that courage is within you, and you will survive and thrive!

Over the course of my life, I've experienced situations that required me to be courageous. I climbed Mt. Rainier (the summit sits at 14, 411 feet). I spent 12 months apart from everyone I knew during my first year of college. I moved a lot (Cambodia to America, Oregon to New York, New York to Oregon, Oregon to Arizona, Arizona to Washington State, and from Eastern Washington to Western Washington.) I moved because the opportunity to learn and create a better life existed. I didn't know that as a toddler leaving Cambodia, but somehow, I believe that experience laid a foundation for me to seek and find something better. And I have. So can you!

Chapter 3
White Out in West Linn

Whatever you did for the least of these, you did for me. –
Jesus Christ

My family relied on each other for everything once we arrived in the U.S. Not only were we in a place vastly different from home, we also didn't understand a lot of what was happening around us. In the wake of this tragic journey, goodness did find its way to the 12 of us. The congregation of the church in West Linn (a suburb of Portland, Oregon) welcomed us with music, a feast, and open arms. We were given food, shelter, and clothing, and as the weeks passed, we learned to communicate with the Pastor and the members of the church enough to survive.

My parents both worked; my mom worked for the church and was able to take care of us each day. As the youngest child, I watched my sisters and brother go off to school one by one, anticipating what being a student would be like for me.

∞∞∞∞

It was finally here! The first day of first grade, and I was in a classroom without my family. I knew some of my classmates from church; however, the elementary school provided me with many new faces to meet.

"Hi. I'm Katy," I said to a group of students. Katy was the "American" name I used back then.

"Hey, you guys, look at her. She looks like chocolate. Let's eat her!" said one of the boys.

That was the first time I recognized that the color of my skin was different from everyone else. There were no other minorities in my elementary school, in the church, or in all of West Linn (I believe). I had never had another human being acknowledge that my skin color was different; moreover, as a six-year-old on the first day of school, I was scared to death because Peter said he wanted to eat me!

I remember spending that day trying to understand why my skin was different from my teacher, my classmates, and everyone around me. When I got home from school, I found a bottle of White-Out® and began to paint my skin. I had most of one arm from elbow to wrist done when my mom asked me what I was doing.

"Sok-Khieng, no!" She took me to the bathroom and used a combination of rubbing alcohol and dish soap to remove my attempt to look like everyone else.

"This is not to play with. Your arm is going to be red and itchy."

"Mama, the kids at school wanted to eat me!" I cried. "They said I look like chocolate candy."

"That's silly. You are overreacting. Always with the drama, this one," said my mom as she continued to scrub.

I still remember that frightened little girl's reaction to my first experience with racism. Although Peter and I became good friends while I was in elementary, my family remained the only non-whites for all my years in school. I don't remember any other incidents like the one from that first day, but somehow, I never felt like I was the same as the rest of my classmates again. My siblings excelled in school; two of my sisters and my brother were valedictorians of their graduation class.

My life in West Linn remained mostly the same during my school years. My parents didn't expect much from me academically, and when I realized that I didn't have to be focused on my grades and studying like they insisted for my siblings, I became more social, had good friends, was a cheerleader in high school, and honestly can say I enjoyed those years. I was growing up as an American in the suburbs of the Pacific Northwest. I knew I was different but had no real understanding of what that meant.

Despite not being pushed to achieve academic success, my grades were good, and I received a full ride scholarship to Hofstra University in Hempstead, New York on Long Island. Okay, it was a dance scholarship, but I was off to earn a college degree! It turns out that New York is really far from Oregon and really lonely when your parents can't afford to visit. I felt like a refugee once again.

∞∞∞

Delighting in Being Different

As adults, being different is often celebrated and admired by others. As a child and teenager, different is often a painful experience and an unhappy memory. The ability to learn and grow from those moments and acknowledge that differences exist for every human defines those moments very differently. If you have those experiences from your past, spend some time recalling the moment and try to reinvent the experience. Peter had no intention of being racist. He was six and my guess is that in his brief lifetime his limited vocabulary and understanding of life caused him to see brown skin and think of chocolate; a tasty treat and a pleasant experience for many. If he knew that the world is made up of human beings with many different skin tones, customs, and abilities, I doubt he would have thought I was edible. His love of chocolate and desire to consume me could be seen as a compliment!

Nevertheless, none of us came to that moment understanding that the exchange was inappropriate.

When my son wanted to wear a shirt in the swimming pool because his skin is different than his friend's, I reminded him that different is okay. He smiled when I mentioned how much we appreciate that he eats the orange jellybeans (only one in the family who likes them) and that was different. He wore his shirt. I like to believe that he made the choice for other reasons; however, I also know we learn from experience. I will continue to remind both my children how special different is.

Part 2
Becoming Me

Chapter 4
A Family of One

Missing someone isn't about how long it has been since there with you." –unknown

The idea that I had earned the opportunity to study at a four-year academic university was awesome. My parents had raised five children by this time, and I still felt like I was proving my

 worthiness to them. I left in the summer for Hofstra, excited to be on the school's dance team, living in a dorm on my own, and studying at the college

level.

I wasn't prepared for very much of what the next 12 months entailed. First, there was a rigorous practice schedule and strict eating and exercise component for the dance team. Next, my class schedule sometimes conflicted with dance team required meetings, and I struggled with being loyal to both my academic and athletic schedules. Finally, my family couldn't afford to visit, nor could I go back to Oregon to see them. My boyfriend from high school, Michael, and I remained a couple, but a long distance relationship, especially with the lack of ways to connect (it was the mid-90s) made our relationship shaky at best.

I think many college freshman experience a lot of what I did. I became friends with several girls at Hofstra,  but I was never really able to express what I was feeling. I don't think I even understood why I felt so alone and abandoned. Yes, my almost three-year-old mind may not have comprehended being exiled from my birthplace, but my 19-year-old self felt the agony of displacement during a time that, although scary and challenging, should also be a time to learn and grow as a human. Instead, I retreated to a dark place inside and decided to return to Oregon and give up on my college degree.

∞∞∞

Understanding Independence

Leaving home for the first time is an exhilarating and scary experience. Nothing prepares us for life alone without parental influence. Sleepovers, summer camp, even long-term visits to auntie's house really don't compare to that first real home that is not the one that is familiar. For me, I was like so many high school seniors, anticipating and excited for college, life without my parents telling me what to do, and the next step to becoming me. And like most, I was unprepared.

Looking back to those days now, I realize that I knew myself better than I thought. Don't get me wrong, that year was difficult. I was really lonely and didn't know how to express my concerns to anyone. But the internal conversations I had with myself were valuable and are lessons I still live by today. I somehow knew that there was no way I was giving up. NO WAY. Even when suicide crossed my mind, I valued myself and the chance I was given to become a part of something big.

Being alone can be hard; however, not reaching out and suffering or harming yourself, is worse. There is ALWAYS someone to talk with. ALWAYS. If you believe that you are without help, call a suicide hotline (in the U.S. 1.800.273.8255), visit a nearby house of worship, or look online for someone to communicate with. YOU ARE WORTH IT!

Chapter 5
Roots: Not Quite Deep Enough

*Don't change yourself so that other people will like you. Be
yourself, and the right people will like you.* -unknown

I left Hofstra University after Spring Quarter
in June 1994. I was looking forward to spending
time with Michael, enjoying my friends and family
still in West Linn, and thinking about what I wanted
to do next.

My family was indifferent with my return
home. I'd heard them say "she doesn't function like
her siblings" throughout my life, and I asked my
mom about it one day.

"The doctors in Thailand said you would be
retarded and would never be able to do what your
siblings could," she expressed with little emotion.
"So we let you play and do your dance and
cheerleader stuff. We didn't want to push you."

"But I got a college scholarship! Does that
sound like I can't learn to you?"

"You are not on scholarship now, Sok-
Khieng." She walked away.

My boyfriend will be there for me, I thought. I left home that day, seeking Michael's comfort. We had plans to meet in the parking lot of the grocery store. When I arrived, he wasn't alone, and he was getting stoned with his friends. I had my mom's car, and he finally got in it to talk to me.

I was really looking forward to sharing about being back in town and being together again. He got in the car and we hugged. "Hey babe, you look good," he said.

"Thanks, Michael. You look wasted."

He smoked pot while we were in high school and apparently hadn't stopped. He laughed and said, "Yeah, I am. Whatcha gonna do about it?"

It didn't take long for me to realize one short year apart changed how I felt about that. "What do you want me to do, Michael? I don't like you smoking pot and being out of it like you are. I wanted to talk and catch up."

"I'm not going to stop smoking marijuana, Sok-Khieng. Why should I?"

I didn't say anything. I just looked at him and he got out of the car and went with his friends. Those were pretty much the last words I ever heard him say.

∞∞∞

Love Can Hurt

My story began more than 7000 miles from where I grew up in Portland, Oregon. Many of my experiences are different from yours. Still, in many ways, my story mirrors that of an average American. My race, religion, hobbies, academic ability, even my gender doesn't matter much when it is in regard to relationships…the romantic ones. Human beings by nature like to coexist with other humans. The pandemic of 2020 is a great example of the frustrating and dysfunctional situation that kept the citizens of earth alone, quarantined for weeks at a time.

I enjoy experiencing life more when I share it with someone else. No one creates the rules for romantic relationships. We seem to make them up as we go through them. There never seems to be much thought about what to do when a relationship has to end. We never think about it. Whether you've had many romantic relationships or just a few, experiencing the end, the loss of that companion, can teach us how to give more to others and take better care of ourselves. Eyes on the prize, I always say. The lesson learned pays off in the end.

Chapter 6
Earning a College Degree

Opportunities don't happen. You create them. -- Chris Grosser

My return home didn't pan out like I had envisioned, so I left for the University of Oregon in Eugene that August. I didn't understand it then, but my year away in New York helped me learn independence and confidence and gave me a  foundation for what it takes to be successful. It really hurt that my high school sweetheart chose the life he did—without me. Still, I managed to move forward and leave the safety of West Linn. Granted, the University of Oregon is less than two hours away compared to the distance of Hofstra (almost 3000 miles). Becoming self-reliant felt like a tough task to achieve at that time of my life. I looked at living on my own as a chore, a result of not being good enough. I was determined though.

I graduated three years later with a psychology degree (with a political science minor) and left Eugene for Arizona to stay with my sister. I was growing up, ready to move forward. Sort of. I had a boyfriend in Eugene, Trey, who was a year behind me in school. He planned to enter the police academy in Portland, Oregon after graduation, and I was going to move to Portland with him. He grew up there and his family lived close by. They looked like the family I wanted for myself. It felt like a solid plan. That didn't work out so well.

After a few months in Arizona, I learned that Trey cheated on me, with one of our good friends. I broke up with him and felt lost and betrayed, not knowing where to go on this journey of life.

∞∞∞∞

Celebrating Our Accomplishments

When you accomplish a goal: graduating from school, learning a trade, getting your first apartment, buying your first car, the world looks awesome. You did it and believe anything is possible. Then reality sets in and you can't find a job, rent is going up, you get in an accident and now you feel the self-doubt and lack of accomplishment again.

I graduated college. I earned a degree that opened up my options. Being cheated on took the joy out of everything that felt good. I enjoyed being in Arizona with my sister and having family with me helped as I worked through my feelings after the breakup. Still, I let a negative take precedence over all the good and exciting things happening in my life. I've learned to appreciate and be grateful for all of life's experiences. And I've learned to be grateful for the positive in my life and focus as best I can on those moments.

Being betrayed doesn't have to create a doubting, cautious, lost person. Give yourself the gift of forgiveness and find the peace to move on. Being grateful for the lessons learned is a better choice than worrying about someone who probably isn't even thinking about you.

Chapter 6 Follow-up—An Old Friend Indeed

Many years later, in 2004, I was living in Western Washington and decided to drive to Portland to see family who still lived in that area. I was crossing one of the many bridges leading into the city and wasn't paying enough attention to the speed I was traveling. The police cruiser behind me was, and I looked in my rearview mirror and saw flashing lights. I pulled over.

Damn, I thought as I fluffed up my hair and unfastened one more button on my blouse. *Maybe he'll take pity on an attractive young woman from out of town.* I smiled and put down the window. "Is there a problem officer?"

"May I see your driver's license, registration, and proof of insurance, please?" said the tall, probably really handsome officer.

I love a man in a uniform, I thought as I turned towards him with the necessary documents.

We spoke each other's names as our eyes recognized one another. "Trey?"

"Sok Khieng?"

It was my boyfriend from the University of Oregon, a police officer for the city of Portland! He fulfilled his dreams and was living the life he'd imagined. I didn't get a speeding ticket and Trey and I met that evening to catch up. It was a great way to let the negative be gone forever!

Chapter 7
Searching in the Grand Canyon

Success seems to be connected with action. Successful people keep moving. They make mistakes, but they don't quit. --
Conrad Hilton

While living with my sister, I took a job as a paralegal for an attorney in Phoenix. Since I minored in Political Science at the University of Oregon, it felt like a good fit. My boss knew what had happened with my relationship in Oregon and suggested I "ditch love" and enroll in law school! It seemed like a good idea, and in August 1997, I began my law studies at the University of Arizona.

During the last year of law school, we were required to complete clinical work, so I joined the immigration law clinic on campus. Since Arizona  is a border state to Mexico, there was a lot of immigration work within the clinic, and I became extremely interested in this specialty of the law. During my tenure with the clinic, I met a border patrol agent, David, and we began dating.

I graduated law school and accepted a

position with the largest law firm in Spokane, Paine Hamblen, and moved to Washington State in May 2000. David and I maintained a long distance relationship. I remembered what happened the last time I tried that, but I felt that I was more mature now and both of us agreed it was worth continuing.

∞∞∞

Experiencing Difference

Reflection leads to growth and usually helps us to move forward and understand life better. I realized that I had been living life as it unfolded and kept myself open to new experiences. I was in my 20s and excited to have my first real job as an attorney. I had moved from Oregon to New York and back again, to Arizona and now to Washington State. I wonder if my early years gave me the incentive to see the world and experience the U.S.A.'s different cultures and lifestyles? I do believe that my adventures helped me be confident and willing to accept a new challenge.

One of the greatest gifts you can give to yourself is to experience differences, to meet people who have had a different experience than you, to see what lies around the corner. It doesn't require an airplane, long distances, or even a car ride. Lift your head, look forward, and see who and what can teach you something new. You will be grateful.

Chapter 8
Not What I Expected

A mind that is stretched by new experiences can never go back to its old dimensions. --Oliver Wendell Holmes, Jr.

I spent one year "east of the mountains" in Washington State. Shortly after moving there, one of the attorneys in the office suggested I visit Coeur de 'Alene, Idaho, a quaint town not far from Spokane.

When I arrived in town, I parked my car and noticed that the streets were empty. I saw activity in the distance, and I realized a parade was taking place and coming my way. *This should be fun,* I thought. I couldn't remember the last time I watched a parade.

As the procession drew nearer, I realized that some of the participants in the parade were dressed in white robes with cone-shaped masks covering their faces. These were members of the Ku Klux Klan, marching down the streets of Coeur de 'Alene, Idaho! I ran my brown-self back to my car and headed back to Spokane.

Much to my dismay, I got lost. I ended up in Hayden Lake, a suburb of Coeur de 'Alene. I didn't know it at the time, but the small town was home to a 20-acre compound of the Aryan Nation, a white supremacist group. The leader of that group, Richard Butler, led the parade that day in the streets of Coeur de 'Alene. The Ku Klux Klan marched with him to support the white supremacist group. Luckily, I made it back to Spokane without any problems.

Looking back at that incident it felt as if I were having an out of body experience when I ran back to my car knowing it was a KKK parade. I had an older model Ford Escort and needed to insert the key to unlock the door. I couldn't find my keys in my purse because my hands were shaking so badly. *How could I have been so naive and ignorant to think there are no longer people who hate someone purely because of the color of their skin?* Part of me wanted to run to my family and law school friends to hug them and live my sheltered, safe life because I knew these people loved me and accepted me for who I was no matter the color of my skin. I finally found my keys and unlocked the car door. As I was trying to navigate my way out of there, two thoughts kept popping into my head: (1) How could hate like this still exist? and (2) Where the hell am I going, and why can't I find my way back to the main highway to Spokane?

 Once I got back to my apartment in Spokane and calmed down, I decided to start studying for the bar and looking ahead. I felt like I needed to build a wall around my emotions and feelings to survive. I needed to be selective as to who I let into my personal space in Spokane. I believe that's why my closest friends from there were a Vietnamese man and an African American man, both attorneys at the firm, whom I believed never would judge me by the color of my skin. It was a horrible way to view life, people, and my colleagues in Spokane, but that was the defense and survival mechanism I created there because my eyes were opened to the reality that white power and hate still were present in 2000 in Coeur de 'Alene, Idaho, too close to my home. I shouldn't have assumed that the other white people I interacted with in Spokane felt the same way as the KKK, but it was such a jarring experience, I couldn't find a way to mentally think they wouldn't judge me by the color of my skin.

I studied for the bar and completed my exam in July 2000. I was sworn in as an attorney in November that same year. I was still uncomfortable living so close to Northern Idaho; nevertheless, I had worked non-stop to earn my degrees and I was passionate about my work, so I persevered.

Then, less than a year later, the event that changed history forever happened: 911. David, my boyfriend, the border patrol agent in Arizona, was hired as an Air Marshall and moved to the Seattle-Tacoma area of Washington to work from the airport. I jumped at the opportunity to leave Spokane and in early 2002, left Paine Hamblen Law Offices to reconnect with David and settle down.

∞∞∞

When Fight or Flight Happens

The state of living with high stress and anxiety is called fight or flight and often is used to describe our ancestors, the cavemen. Think about living in a cave and deciding to take a walk around the neighborhood. I'm sure the scenery was lovely, without pollution or garbage or concrete skyscrapers to block the view. You might find peace and solace while walking along quietly. All of a sudden, you hear rustling in the distance and turn around to see a sabretooth tiger running your way!

Fight or flight kicks in and because you left your shotgun at home (oops, those didn't exist at the time), you begin running, hoping to make it back to the cave and push the rock back to block the entrance before the tiger arrives to have her lunch.

How different was my KKK/Aryan experience from being chased by a sabretooth tiger, really? My life could have been in danger. I wasn't prepared for what I had encountered so fight wasn't an option. Have you ever run away to avoid a situation? Have you ever stayed and fought? Were either of those choices the right solution?

We have the ability to let go of the fight or flight approach to life and live in the present moment, fully engaged and enjoying life. That doesn't mean you can ignore the laws and guidelines that keep the world safe and livable. But sabretooth tigers and most other life-threatening situations don't exist anymore. We have ways to get away from danger and avoid it in the first place. There really isn't a need to live life always looking for danger and dread. That doesn't mean "bad things" don't happen. How you deal with them in the moment and when you process the situation do. Find the gifts. Find peace and love.

Chapter 9
A Place to Call Home

It's not the days in your life, but the life in your days that counts. —Brian White

My boyfriend and I were establishing a life together in Renton, WA, just south of Seattle. I interviewed with and was hired by the law firm of Davies Pearson in Tacoma, WA. I began there in March 2002 and spent much of my career with one of the premiere law firms in the area. Life felt settled, exciting, and everything I could have imagined. Until...

David had applied for and was accepted to the FBI without my knowledge. He assumed I would join him in Quantico, VA, where he would receive training. I'd made too many decisions based more on someone else than I cared to acknowledge. I really loved him but couldn't do it again. We parted ways in 2003.

I spent the next several years focused on my work as an immigration attorney, learning all I could about what other facets of the law were of interest to me. I became a partner and a shareholder at Davies Pearson in 2008, and I began working with personal injury cases, an area of law that has become my true calling. I love assisting people, getting to know them as more than clients, and finding ways to help them thrive.

I had the chance to visit Cambodia in November 2009. My mom and my sister, Sokie, and I flew from Seattle to Phnom Penh, Cambodia. This was my sister's and my first time back to Cambodia. My mother, father, and three other siblings had visited Cambodia on numerous occasions. When we got there, we met up with my oldest sister, Sally, her husband, Sarady, and their children, Collin, Kaitlyn, and Kyle, who were already in Cambodia visiting Sarady's family.

We stayed in Phnom Penh for two days before making our way to the city of Siem Reap in Northern Cambodia to visit Angkor Wat, a complex of Buddhist temples originally built as a Hindu temple in the 12th century. It was amazing. We stayed at Siem Reap for four days then headed south to the village where we were born in the province of Kampot.

I was struck how some villages/towns were still very much like a third world country, with

homes built on bamboo sticks with no modernized restrooms. Other towns were

42

very commercialized places, and at that time, it appeared that there were many Korean and Chinese investors there, and Cambodia was losing its rich, cultural, national identity.

We were able to visit my mom's and dad's side of the family. Both of my parents had eight siblings each, and we had 60 plus cousins still living there. My relatives all thought my sister and I were "old hags" because we were not married, had no kids, and were in our 30s. I was okay being labeled an old hag as I was  not ready to settle down or have kids in 2009!

I went to Cambodia with two oversized suitcases, a duffle bag, and a carry on filled with clothes, shoes, make-up, a hair dryer, curling irons and other necessities a girl like me needs to travel with. When I boarded the plane to come back to the U.S., I only had a plastic grocery bag with trinkets I bought from the street market as my relatives wanted everything I had, even worn underwear, bras, and my used toothbrush! They had access to so little and I gladly gave them my "treasures," no matter how little I thought they meant.

I realized that there is so much of the world that I would like to see. I know that Cambodia is the place where I was born and someday, I would like my husband and kids to visit it. I would like to explore other parts of the world like Ireland and Italy as well.

Life on the west side of the mountain (Mt. Rainier) has much to offer, and I enjoyed many social aspects of my new home. In 2008, I joined a dragon boat club and became a member of the

Tacoma Nagas team. Many of the members were Cambodian, and we supported troubled youths in the area, working to help them find focus and purpose while keeping them actively involved in health and fitness. I loved the diversity of the group, and really enjoyed the camaraderie of the team.

One of my teammates invited his college roommate to join us. Tyler Hardy and I met in the Spring of 2009. He is ten years younger than I, was raised in Washington, and other than paddling the same dragon boat together, was nothing like I am.

Still, we have been married since 2012 and are raising a family together!

∞∞∞

Loving Yourself to Love Others

I spent years dating partners I believed were the perfect match for me. From my first serious relationship in high school (okay, serious for a teenager!) to the FBI agent, my choices were based more on an ideal than reality. When we become friends and romantic partners with another person, it is so easy to become complacent and forget why we began the relationship in the first place. When you stop taking care of yourself and expect someone else to take care of your needs for you, relationships don't work out too well. For me, I was "single" for several years after David moved to Virginia and for the first time, really learned to love myself. I think that period of growth and self-care laid the foundation for my strong and loving connection with Tyler.

Self-care is the first step to a successful and fulfilling relationship with another person. Think about it. Would you want to date yourself? If you really love who you are, the answer is obvious. On the other hand, if the answer is no, ask yourself why anyone else would want to be your partner. Remember to love yourself always!

Part 3

Being Me

Chapter 10
A Celebration Across Cultures

Love can come when you're already who you are when you're filled with you. Not when you look to someone else to fill the empty space. – Deb Caletti

Tyler and I complement each other in many ways because of our differences. He encourages me to pursue my goals and keeps me motivated when I need a little shove (or a major kick in the butt).

I spent several years focused on my career and my personal growth, and the idea of settling down was far from my thoughts when Tyler and I first met. I'd dated several guys since arriving in the area, and I was content keeping things non-committal. When Tyler asked me out, I declined more than once, mostly because of our age difference. He persisted though, and in August of 2009, we made a vow to date each other exclusively. We got engaged in early 2012 and set our wedding date for early August that same year.

Looking back on that time period, I am amazed that we accomplished what we did in the course of a few months. In addition to a wedding ceremony and reception in downtown Seattle for 250 guests, we had a combination Cambodian/Chinese ceremony the day before, and we managed to train for and climb Mt. Rainier (14,411 feet)! We had a huge photo of Tyler and me on the summit adorning the entrance to our wedding venue. It was a beautiful and meaningful part of that day.

Our wedding days were lovely. Asian weddings are filled with many different ceremonies and are steeped in tradition. We opted for two simple ceremonies (Chinese for my mom and Cambodian for my dad) the day before our

American wedding. We invited our family and close friends to our house for the weddings. We had a huge Asian feast. I remember that I was nervous that some of my Cambodian relatives might think the pets there that day (dog is a cuisine in Cambodia) were for the feast! Thank God I was being silly! Later that evening, we went to Seattle to decorate the venue for the American celebration. We also had a rehearsal dinner that evening in Seattle!

It was 90 degrees outside, and aside from a broken air conditioner in the men's limo and a slightly inebriated bridesmaid, our large wedding party (eight groomsmen, eight bridesmaids, and one junior bridesmaid) and a multitude of friends and family had a great time celebrating the beginning of what has been a special and invaluable relationship to me.

During the reception, my father quieted the crowd to make a toast. This was not part of the well-planned day, and my Cambodian father's command of English was not at the toastmaster level! When my brother-in-law Sarady, a colonel in the U.S. Air Force joined him, I realized that Dad would speak Khmer and Sarady would translate to English. Afterall, our marriage brought these two cultures together that day to celebrate and now everyone would understand his words.

Many of you here today know Sok-Khieng as a beautiful, successful woman who brings joy and love to those around her. When we left Cambodia in 1978 to escape what was happening in our homeland, Sok-Khieng was barely three years old. We had to travel to Thailand with more than 100 others in a small wooden boat designed for about 50 adults.

Because of the fear of being heard and seen, we left Cambodia in the middle of the night, doing our best to keep the young children on board silent. As we slowly floated toward the shore of Thailand, Sok-Khieng fell into the water. I got in the water and somehow managed to find her in the darkness. We were close enough to the boarder that she was able to be revived and then examined by the doctors at the camp where we were taken before we were sent to the United States.

Tyler and Sok-Khieng, you two are not supposed to be together for many different reasons. But as I raise my glass to toast you this evening, I am so incredibly grateful that you have found each other and wish you happiness, peace, and love for many years to come. Congratulations, I love you both.

I was astounded! I knew that many of the guests in the room had no idea that I was not born in the United States. Even Tyler didn't know about what had happened on the boat when my family left Cambodia. At first, I was embarrassed. I imagined my "white friends" either feeling sorry for me or teasing me about being a refugee. But, as I looked around the room that day, I realized that I was the only one reacting negatively. People were dabbing their eyes. Moreover, my Cambodian family members were sitting taller, obviously proud to celebrate my accomplishments and their own achievements as citizens not born in America.

As human beings, we have many reasons to celebrate each other's lives. I received a gift that day that continues to remind me how special life is.

∞∞∞

A Life Worth Living

What about you do you think of as an embarrassment? It may be a habit, an experience from childhood, a physical difference, or other things that, when thought about by someone other than you, have no reason to be embarrassing or negative. Life is about being ourselves, and if we were all the same, how could we celebrate being special? When I watch the video of our wedding day, I feel pride; I am a

53

Cambodian born American wife, mother, friend, and citizen whose experiences have made me who I am today.

We miss out on so much because of the time (for some that can be a lifetime) we spend resisting the world around us. As children, we have no real understanding of what prejudice means. By "old age" most of us just don't care. It's the rest of life…the majority of life…that gets tangled in our self-inflicted fears and judgments of others. Let us all be the child or be the elder and live a life worth living.

Chapter 11
Babies and Blessings

There are many things in life that will catch your eye, but only a few will catch your heart. Pursue these.

–Michael Nolan

Our firstborn, Wyatt, arrived seven months after Tyler and I married. We wanted to have children right away, but his conception was not one of my best-laid plans! I like to call this our Aunt Flo story:

It was a week before the wedding, and Tyler and I were at Red Robin having dinner and discussing wedding plans.

"Ya know hon, Aunt Flo hasn't visited recently, and I was counting on her appearance, so she doesn't show up at the wedding. (Aunt Flo is what I call my menstrual cycle.) I must be stressed about all there still is left to do."

"Do you think you could be pregnant?"

"No way! We're careful. We didn't use anything that one time, but I was having my...you know, Aunt Flo was in town."

"I'm not sure that counts as birth control, honey. Let's get a pregnancy test on the way back to your place. Just in case."

"Fine, but I'm not pregnant."

We stopped at Rite Aid and got a pregnancy test. We were in the bathroom, and as I'm holding a stick and peeing on it, Tyler is brushing his teeth and reading the directions for the test.

"What does two lines mean?" I asked.

I heard the toothbrush hit the sink and the father of my children was staring at me as foam was dripping down the sides of his mouth. His eyes said it all. He confirmed it as he said, "Holy shit! We're pregnant."

I knew then that Aunt Flo wouldn't be at the wedding, on our honeymoon, or in our lives for quite a while. I can't believe I really thought I couldn't get pregnant when I was having my period. Some lessons learned are quite the surprise!

Wyatt's presence in our lives is a gift we are grateful for every day. He is a sweetheart. He is quiet, kind, and very much a perfect combination of Tyler and me. We didn't want to wait long to give him a sibling and began planning for a second child. Unfortunately, conventional methods for conception weren't cooperating with our timeline and Wyatt's sibling's story is quite different than his surprising conception.

∞∞∞

We decided to enlist the aid of a fertility clinic after months of following all the guidelines to conceive and not becoming pregnant. We began with the I.U.I. (Intrauterine Insemination) process. Every month I would have Tyler's best cleaned and prepped sperm injected directly into my uterus. Six of those procedures and nothing, so we took the next step of invitro fertilization, where my eggs were raised outside my body. Of the two viable eggs we created, one of them "took" and now Wyatt was going to be a big brother!

For anyone who has experienced infertility, there is little beauty in the moments of clinical and regulated conception; and as the expert at compartmentalizing every aspect of life I could, I put the pregnancy in the file cabinet of my brain as "accomplished" and moved on with life. I had a toddler at home and had become a partner with the law firm. We were busy, grateful for the resources we had to have a second child, and focused on the pending birth and true joy children bring.

I was the last one in the office. It was about 6:15 p.m., and I felt a wetness on my chair. I got up to investigate and realized that I was bleeding profusely and headed quickly to the bathroom. I was 12 weeks pregnant. When I sat on the toilet, I felt a small mass coming, so I put my hand between my legs. I was holding what I assumed was my unborn child. Without thinking too much, I wrapped it in toilet paper, cleaned myself up, made certain the bathroom was cleaned, and called my obstetrician to ask what to do. Then I called Tyler to tell him what was happening.

"Come home now." He sounded shaky at best.

My doctor told me to keep the mass in the refrigerator in a plastic bag and to bring it to his office the next day. He needed to examine it before concluding that I had a miscarriage.

Tyler and Wyatt were there when I arrived home, and we sat on the couch trying not to think about what was in the refrigerator. It was a long night.

We went to the doctor the next day and received confirmation that the mass was a 12 week old fetus. I had had a miscarriage. I was told to come back for a D&C the next day if I was still bleeding. The D&C would clean my uterus and help avoid infection from the blood loss and the pregnancy itself.

We called our family and some friends that evening to share our news. It wasn't until the two of us sat with Wyatt to explain what happened that I finally cried. Too many events have happened in my life that could be called tragedies, yet nothing ever felt as painful as that moment. I felt like I'd failed as a woman, not being able to carry my child to full term. Wyatt really didn't understand the scope of the situation, yet he comforted us as much as we did him that evening.

I went in the next morning because the bleeding was still heavy. The technician handed me a gown to change into for the D&C. He got the sonogram machine ready to see the tissue and any damage there might be in my uterus. He moved the wand around on my lower abdomen and looked at the monitor.

"Are you here for a D&C, Sok Khieng?"

"Yes. I miscarried the other night."

"I'm not sure what happened but there is a fetus inside your uterus. Listen."

I heard my daughter's heartbeat.

The technician showed me a fetus that measured just about two inches. I never had the D&C that day, and Whitney was born 24 weeks later! My doctor did confirm that her twin was stillborn at 12 weeks. My elation that day and the joy and blessings that Whitney brings to our lives is a gift I will be grateful for always.

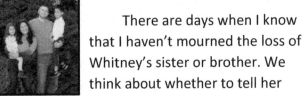

There are days when I know that I haven't mourned the loss of Whitney's sister or brother. We think about whether to tell her about what happened. Life is too short to fixate on the negatives, but we don't want to dismiss the loss of life either. To all the women who have miscarried, you are and will always be a whole woman who has and will continue to make this world a better place for you, your family, and your community. Whitney is the shining star that reminds me every day how precious and lucky we all are to be alive.

∞∞∞

The Value of the Relationship

The relationships in our lives deserve to take precedence. Okay, how do we determine which relationship gets to be the priority? Parenthood often involves more than one child so how do you prioritize multiple relationships? Add to the mix a job, a partner, parents, siblings, friends, and yourself and the word priority loses its punch.

When I look at my two children, I see many connections. We are a family of four. I am a mom to two. I am also a mom of a third child who doesn't exist in this world, yet I feel maternal feelings for him/her and always will. I see my relationship as a mother to my son differently than to my daughter. I realize that's not only because they are different genders but are different people and their personalities reflect our connections to each other.

My other relationships: wife, friend, lawyer, mentor, sibling, child, are invaluable to my existence. We each have connections with others that shape who we are as humans. The one commonality to them is the value placed on the relationship itself. To gain from it, giving must be part of it in order to consider it a successful relationship. It is through giving that we are able to see each of our relationships as being the most important. Knowing that we are all connected takes the need out of seeing them as separate.

The most valuable lesson I can share with you is the importance of your relationship with yourself. In order to be a great parent, wife, child, sibling, or friend you need to love

61

yourself. Take time every day for self-care. There will be days when time permits a spa treatment or a cup of tea and a good book. Other days may only allow for a few deep breaths and a reminder of how important you are. No matter the event, take the time to take care of you. All of your relationships will thank you.

Chapter 12
Reflections of the Future

I was always looking outside myself for strength and confidence, but it comes from within. It is there all the time.

-Anna Freud

Part of me has always wanted to write a book to reflect on my life and the lessons I've learned from my experiences, but the last few years have made me feel a sense of urgency to share my story with the world.

I am a refugee. I am fresh off the boat, literally. Always have been and a part of me always will be, and that's okay. It's okay to have this refugee beginning and be an American simultaneously. I support the Constitution of the United States. I have and would again take the Oath of Allegiance. I would bear arms for this country. I am as American as any other American, but with a different set of circumstances and background that led me to be who I am today. I am proud to be an American.

I would love to say that the world reflects my philosophy completely. Unfortunately, I still encounter situations that say differently. In 2018, I was driving to Lynnwood (north of Seattle) to meet with an expert in a case on which I was working. It was after Donald Trump's inauguration in 2017 and a memo had been issued by Jeff Sessions, the Attorney General of the United States at the time, which basically informed the Department of Homeland Security not to believe the credibility of asylum seekers. Furthermore, local and state law enforcement agencies received a memo to report all illegal aliens to the Immigration & Customs Enforcement Unit if they suspected someone was an undocumented person in the United States. Something told me to put my passport (proof of my citizenship) in my purse. I did. That act saved me that day I was driving to Lynnwood.

I was going 40 mph in a 25 mph zone as I was running late, so it wasn't a surprise that I heard a siren and saw flashing lights in my rear view mirror. I was getting pulled over by the Washington State Patrol. I fully expected to get a ticket and deserved it because I was speeding. He came to my window and asked for my license and registration, which I handed him, and he went back to his car. He came back to my window, and I assumed he would have a speeding ticket for me. However, he said, "I'm going to need to see proof of your legal status, Miss."

"Pardon me?" I said, stunned by the question.

"May I see proof that you have legal status in the U.S.?" he repeated.

I remembered my passport and turned towards my purse to retrieve it. I paused, turned towards him, and asked, "Why do I need to show you proof of my legal status?"

He said, "I'm asking the questions here." His tone was not very pleasant.

At this point, the defiant, aggressive me came out and I knew I might be in trouble if I said something rude, but this was wrong on so many levels. I turned to him and said, "Okay," and I reached into my purse and grabbed my U.S. passport. As I handed it to him, I added, "I'm also going to give you my business card as I'm an immigration attorney, and if you do run into anyone who is undocumented, I may be able to help them get legal status."

He was the one who looked stunned now. He seemed flustered as he looked at my U.S. passport and business card, then handed those back to me along with the other documents of mine he had and told me that I could go.

You would think I would be celebrating because I didn't get a speeding ticket, but I wasn't. I was so infuriated and scared because I was thinking that if I hadn't had my passport in my purse, there was no way I could show the guy I had legal status to be in the U.S. Not many citizens would know that they could be questioned about their status, let alone show proof as such.

Even though I was driving a year old Mercedes Benz GL450, spoke crystal clear English, and was dressed in a business suit because I was working, I was treated poorly. It was another reminder to me what a divisive world we were living in under the current government. People clearly have their racist ideology exhibited without fear or embarrassment. In the past, they knew to keep those racist behaviors or thoughts at bay or tempered. I felt betrayed. The police officer's uniform gave him rights that were anything but right!

We live in a country racially divided and saturated with COVID-19 cases. I never imagined that I would see the day where parts of the U.S. shutdown due to a global pandemic, but it did. I know we'll work our way out of this crisis and thrive once again as a nation. The whole world is going through a reset. This is just another moment in my life where a curve ball has caused me to adjust to the moment.

I'm in the middle of yet another change in my life. My commitment to helping others has led me to join the law firm of Rush, Hannula, Harkins, and Kyler in Tacoma, Washington. Their practice is solely personal injury law, and I am confident that my purpose in life will be best utilized there. The majority of my career has been with Davies Pearson, and I leave with sadness knowing I won't be seeing the good friends I've worked with for the last two decades. Nevertheless, my passion to be a voice for those in need led me to my new employer. Truly, I am grateful for the opportunity. It is yet another reminder of how lucky we are to be American and to choose freely our path in life.

I wanted to write a book to document significant aspects of my life and now that this process is nearly complete, I realize what I value most and why. As an attorney who practices personal injury law, I see and hear the worst that can happen when an accident or incident occurs, and the injury is as severe as death or permanent disfigurement. It has a catastrophic impact on family and friends. My client's lives are permanently changed in seconds because of that accident and/or incident. When it's a case involving a child with bad injuries, I find that I rush home to hug my kids and am thankful they are alive and healthy. Moreover, when it's a spouse who has been injured, I call Tyler to hear his voice and know that he's safe and healthy. I find myself living in the moment more so than ever before because at any moment I could die, or I could be permanently injured where I won't be able to communicate or love my family and friends the way I have or want. This book is my message to my children in case I let life get in the way of telling them how much they mean to me.

Sometimes I wake up feeling my life is complete, then my almighty, drama-infested, revolutionary five-year-old daughter will say or do something to remind me how precious every day is. The other day she lectured me about not twisting the peanut butter jar cap too tight because it causes the peanut butter to go dry and not taste fresh! She makes me realize how blessed I am to be raising these little people into adults who will keep me on my toes until the day I die. It is wonderful.

Yes, there are moments of tragedy, horror, regret, and embarrassments we wish would not have happened in our life. However, it's during those times that we thrive and become better than who we were before the experience. I am a better me because of those moments and hope you realize you are a better you because of the bad and the good moments. The me of today will be a different, better, more fulfilled me in the years to come. I know it and I can't wait to experience all the moments along the way.

So blessed am I: refugee, American, me.

Acknowledgements

Because I don't like talking about myself, the thought of writing a book about my journey from Cambodia to the U.S. was unappealing; therefore, I must give credit to Brian Ebersole who continued to prod me to write this book for years. I'm glad I did it, so thank you Brian. I also want to thank Maribeth Slovasky for listening and capturing my words, my emotions, and my life in co-writing this book with me. To my friend, T.J. Pietz, you are wonderful, and your support means a lot to me regarding feedback on this book. To my husband and best friend,

Tyler Hardy, your conservative, black and white engineer rationale perspective helped ground the liberal side of me during the writing of this book, and I love you for that babe! To my siblings, Say P. Tan, Kim P.  Lim, Sanh Chiet Lim, Sok-Leng Lim, and brother-in-law, Sarady Tan, you helped foster who I have become over the years, and I draw strength from our close family love. And to my parents, life threw you a crazy curveball when you were forced to flee the only country you knew, but you survived and raised five wonderful children in the United States who know and understand the importance of thriving and giving back to those in need. Thank you everyone!!

Made in the USA
Las Vegas, NV
10 May 2021

22789112R00049